UNIT 1

God Gives Us Friends

Parenting your 5-Year-Old

Dear Parent or Guardian,

We welcome you and your five-year-old to Sadlier's *Discovering God's Love*.

Know that you have our support and encouragement as you lead your child into a community experience of spiritual and social development. As the Catholic Church teaches, "Parents are 'by word and example the first heralds of the faith with regard to their children'" (*Catechism of the Catholic Church*, 1656).

> "Be imitators of God, as beloved children, and live in love, as Christ loved us."
>
> *Ephesians 5:1-2*

How can parents fulfill their roles as "first heralds of the faith" for their children? They do this first of all by being good parents, the primary providers of nourishment, warmth, rest, and security for their children. This loving care is, for children, a concrete sign of God's love. In their everyday care and concern, parents also provide for needs beyond the physical. As the late Joseph Cardinal Bernardin stated in his book, *Growing in Wisdom, Age and Grace,* "While nurturing human values, such as security and trust, the parent at the same time lays the foundation for religious values, such as the love of God and dependence on God's care."

Supporting parents in laying such a foundation is the goal of this faith-development program for kindergartners. The aim of the program is to articulate and reinforce what is happening each day at home, where faith is spoken of and lived. As Cardinal Bernardin reminded us, "Formal programs of religious formation are important helps, yet they can only supplement the child's experience of living in a Christian home. Programs cannot replace parents in the religious formation of children."

May the grace of the Holy Spirit be with us as we begin this shared experience of faith.

The Sadlier Family

Additional Parenting Resources

Bernardin, Joseph Cardinal. *Growing in Wisdom, Age and Grace: A Guide for Parents in the Religious Education of Their Children.* New York: William H. Sadlier, Inc., 1997.

Nolte, Dorothy Law and Rachel Harris. *Children Learn What They Live: Parenting to Inspire Values.* New York: Workman Publishing Company, Inc. 1998.

Taffel, Ron and Melinda Blau. *Nurturing Good Children Now: 10 Basic Skills to Protect and Strengthen Your Child's Core Self.* New York: Golden Books, 1999.

At Home with Your Family

During the year, you will receive four of these special *Unit Pages* planned around the changing seasons of the year. These pages also introduce the lesson themes in both their spiritual and social aspects.

The four *Unit Pages* will also offer you some insights into the normal developmental changes you can anticipate as your child grows and changes this year. A list of resources is included to help you further develop your parenting skills.

The goal of Unit 1, "God Gives Us Friends," is to help your child to feel warmly welcomed in kindergarten. From the first day of "big school," each child's self-esteem, growing independence, and emerging abilities are affirmed and encouraged. A growing awareness of self as a baptized child of God is an essential goal of the entire program. In the first unit, developing the social skills needed to accept others as gifts of God and friends is emphasized. All of us "discover God's love" in the love we share with others as family, friends, and Church community.

In Unit 1, the children will explore essential attitudes that lead to friendship with others: kindness, helpfulness, and trust. They will be encouraged to adopt these attitudes as their own in everyday situations. In this way, the building blocks of Christian moral development are firmly put in place.

For Storytime During Unit One

Aliki. *We Are Best Friends.* New York: William Morrow & Co., 1991.

Anglund, Joan Walsh. *A Friend Is Someone Who Likes You.* San Diego, CA: Harcourt Brace & Company, 1983.

Carle, Eric. *Do You Want to Be My Friend?* New York: HarperCollins Children's Books, 1987.

Heine, Helme. *Friends.* New York: Simon & Schuster Children's Books, 1986.

_____ . *Best Friends.* New York: Simon & Schuster Children's Books, 1991.

Jahn-Clough, Lisa. *My Friend and I.* Boston: Houghton Mifflin Company, 1999.

Petty, Kate. *Making Friends.* Hauppauge, New York: Barron's Educational Series, Inc., 1991.

Big School

Yesterday was a big day for Joey.
It was his first day in kindergarten!

The teacher met him at the door. "Hello, Joey!" she said as she pinned on his name tag. "I'm Mrs. Cummins. I'll be your teacher this year. Why don't you sit down at this table right here and help your table friends to work on this puzzle?"

Joey's table friends were already busy at work. "My name's Emily," said the girl next to him. "You know what we get to do in kindergarten?"

"What?" asked Joey.

"We get to be line leaders and go to gym! And we can have library time, just like the big kids."

"Does anyone have a small red piece?" asked a boy at the other end of the table.

"I do!" answered Joey. Then Joey put the last puzzle piece where it belonged. Together he and his new friends had made a beautiful picture of a sailboat on a sunny day.

"Yes!" they all called out at the very same time. "We finished the puzzle!"

"Yes," thought Joey to himself. "Kindergarten is going to be fun."

Why do you think kindergarten is going to be fun?

5

Parenting your 5-Year-Old

New Beginnings

Even if your child is a preschool veteran, kindergarten marks a new beginning. Kindergarten, while still considered the last part of preschool, is, in every sense, "big school," as it has come to be called in early childhood circles. The kindergarten year is a very significant one, as it is a direct preparation—socially and academically—for the elementary school experiences ahead.

Socially, five-year-olds are at the best possible stage in life to benefit from the challenges and responsibilities of kindergarten. Years of parental guidance and nurturing have given them the self-confidence they need to approach new people and new situations with genuine interest. Buoyed by this confidence, they welcome every chance to learn, to do, to shine, and to share their particular gifts with others.

> "See, I am doing something new!
> Now it springs forth, do you
> not perceive it?"
>
> Isaiah 43:19

A kindergarten environment is electric with projects and possibilities. Affirmed as individuals, children are ready to contribute to the group as friends, helpers, decision-makers, negotiators of plans and ideas. From the point of view of faith development, five-year-olds exult in God's gifts of family, school, friends, and parish, and are eager to find their place in the world God has given them in love.

Their newest place in this world is the kindergarten room. Make every effort to respond to invitations to "parent nights" or other parent activities. Your new kindergartner will have lots to say and share about the kindergarten day, and you will have a better idea of the subject matter if you have seen the territory!

At Home with Your Family

This is the first of many *Parenting Pages* you will receive after a lesson has been completed. The aim of the *Parenting Page* is to enable parents to extend the theme of the lesson at home. The Scripture quotation on this page reflects this theme and can be shared or prayed at home. This section, "At Home with Your Family," adds home activities to the lesson presented to the group. Usually a craft or baking project and a song that your child learned in the group are presented on this page.

In this lesson, your child was introduced to kindergarten and helped to experience a sense of belonging. Each child made a name badge to wear proclaiming "I'm in kindergarten!" The Sign of the Cross was presented as a sign of God's love and will be prayed in every lesson in the coming year. As this prayer is so central to Catholics as an expression of faith, you may want to review it at home, perhaps at meals or at bedtime prayer. Remind your child that as Catholics we pray the Sign of the Cross to begin and end our prayers.

On the back of this page is the *Read to Me* page from the text. You may want to reread the story with your child, or ask your child to tell you the story from the illustrations. In this lesson's story, Joey's first day in kindergarten is described. How does it compare to your child's first day?

The songs on this page present the theme of the lesson in simple words set to familiar tunes. Your child will already have sung the song presented here in the group. You need not have a perfectly tuned singing voice to enjoy sharing a song like this with your child.

My New Friends

Take a 4″ x 10″ piece of white construction paper. Fold it into four equal parts. With a black marker draw a simple outline of a child's body with hands and feet outstretched. Then help your child cut out the pattern to make a row of new friends holding hands. Glue them outstretched onto a piece of colored construction paper. Print the names of some of your child's new kindergarten friends on the figures. Invite him or her to tell you about these new friends.

My New Friends

(*To the tune of "Where Is Thumbkin?"*)

There is *(friend's name)*.	We belong together
There is *(friend's name)*.	In our kindergarten.
He's (She's) my friend.	Let's be friends.
He's (She's) my friend.	Let's be friends.

UNIT 2
Wonderfully Made by God

Parenting your 5-Year-Old

Mutual Admiration Society

Your five-year-old is beginning kindergarten and is becoming more independent. At the same time, you may have noticed an accompanying appreciation and open admiration of you as mom or dad, especially if you are the primary caregiver. In fact, your five-year-old seems not to be able to get enough of you!

This is the time to graciously accept your role as the most important person in your child's life. As mom, your child orbits around you as the planets orbit the sun. As dad, you are the hero, the best of all possible dads. At times, this open admiration can become annoying (especially when you might be feeling your feet of clay). Try not to let your annoyance show. Leaving an impression of being pushed away can be very detrimental to your child's ongoing development. In purely natural terms, your child is being imprinted with your concerns, your values, your particular way of being human—just as ducklings learn to be ducks by following *their* parents around. Nothing can substitute for this kind of hands-on, in-your-face, underfoot learning. Your child is paying you the utmost compliment in wanting to be just like you.

Grandparents have a large share in this mutual admiration society, and all generations benefit from contact with one another by phone, photo, and visits. If grandparents are at a distance, an adoptive grandparent program may widen your family's circle and brighten an elder's life.

> "Be imitators of God, as beloved children, and live in love."
> *Ephesians 5:1–2*

Now is the time when your child's imitative skills are at their peak. As parents, you are role models, the most important your child will ever have. Above basketball players or teachers or celebrities, your child looks up to *you*. This is also true at the spiritual level. Saint Paul the Apostle considered himself a "father in Christ Jesus" to his new converts and wrote, "Be imitators of me" (I Corinthians 4:16). Your child will imitate you—your language, your attitudes, your prayers, your way of following Christ. Be lavish with praise when your five gets it right. Your child needs praise for success and accomplishments in order for self-esteem and self-confidence to grow. Keep the *mutual* in the mutual admiration society!

Additional Parenting Resources

Ames, Louise Bates and Frances L. Ilg. *Your Five Year Old.* New York: Dell Publishing Company, Inc., 1981.

Friel, John and Linda. *The Seven Worst Things Parents Do.* Deerfield Beach, FL: Health Communications, Inc., 1999.

Halmo, Joan. *Celebrating the Church Year with Young Children.* Collegeville, MN: The Liturgical Press, 1988.

Catholic Household Blessings and Prayers. Washington, D.C.: National Conference of Catholic Bishops, 1989.

At Home with Your Family

The goal of Unit 2 is to provide the children with opportunities to discover the wonders of God's creation, both in living and non-living things, and to see all of creation as a gift to us from God our loving Father.

How wonderfully made by God each of us is will be a theme explored throughout the unit. Children will be encouraged to see themselves as unique individuals made and loved by God. Each of the lessons will help the children develop a strong sense of self-esteem and self-worth.

The children will come to know Jesus Christ as the greatest of all God's gifts to us. They will learn that in God's plan for our world, God gave us his own Son, Jesus, to show us how to love God and others.

The changing seasons and the coming of winter will be highlighted in this unit. Building on the theme of change and growth, the children will explore the changes experienced in the cycle of birth, life, and death. What signs of winter in your area can you help your child experience?

For Storytime During Unit Two

Aliki. *Feelings.* New York: William Morrow & Company, 1986.

Bang, Molly Garrett. *When Sophie Gets Angry—Really, Really Angry . . .* New York: Scholastic, Inc., 1999.

Curtis, Jamie Lee. *Today I Feel Silly and Other Moods That Make My Day.* New York: HarperCollins Publishers, Inc., 1998.

Norac, Carl. *I Love You So Much.* New York: Bantam Doubleday Dell Books for Young Readers, 1998.

_____. *I Love to Cuddle.* New York: Bantam Doubleday Dell Books for Young Readers, 1999.

See What I Can Do!

What wonderful things I can do!
Tell a story about each picture.
Finish the words.

I can play ball.

(fold)

I can climb .

I can ride .

I can _____.

Draw what you can do best.
Tell the story of your drawing.

People are the best part of all that God made.
God loves us.
We can do many things that God can do.
We can love. We can learn.
We can know God.
Show how happy you are to be loved by God.
Finish the words.
Cut out and fold. Make a booklet.

(fold)

I can love .

I can learn .

I am loved by God.

I can know God.

We pray.
Thank you, God, for making us so wonderful! Amen.

Favorite Things to Do

Alex could do many wonderful things. Here are some of the things he liked to do best. See whether you can guess why they were his favorite things to do.

Alex liked to eat pizza. He liked the tangy white cheese, the sweet sausage, the spicy tomato sauce, and the thick crust on the bottom. Whenever he thought of pizza, Alex said, "Yummy!" He liked the way pizza *tasted*.

Alex liked to look at his baby sister whenever he came near her crib. She smiled and waved her arms in the air. That made Alex feel good. He liked *seeing* her play.

Alex liked to hear the roar of a plane's engines when it flew overhead in the sky above his house. He wanted to be on every plane that roared over his head. He liked *hearing* the planes.

Alex liked to touch the warm fur on his cat's back. The cat's fur was soft and smooth. Alex was sure this was the finest cat in the world. Alex liked *touching* his cat's soft fur.

Alex liked to visit the lumberyard with his dad. Even with his eyes closed, he knew when he was near the lumberyard. Alex liked the way wood *smelled*.

God gave us our five senses—to taste, to see, to hear, to touch, and to smell. That's how Alex found his favorite things to do.

What are your favorite things to taste, to see, to hear, to touch, and to smell?
Who gives us all of our favorite things to do?
Who gives us our five senses?

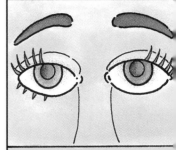

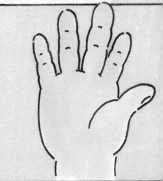

Just Child's Play?

In the past several years, both parents and educators have been almost overwhelmed with research on child development that suggests how very ready to learn young children are. The curriculum for kindergarten is now more academically focused, and parents may wonder whether ordinary playtime should now take the back burner to more formal learning.

> "See what love the Father has bestowed on us that we may be called the children of God."
>
> *1 John 3:1*

A balanced approach is probably the best course. It is important to respect play as central to every level of a child's development. For a young child, there is no distinction between "work" and "play." The alphabet paper presents one kind of challenge; the block corner presents another. The first challenge is that of representing reality with symbols; the second is that of reality itself. Children are faced with the realities of physics and geometry years before they face them in symbols.

Dramatic play, that is, acting out scenes from TV, movies, or real life (the most entertaining of all) is especially important for five-year-olds. It is through this kind of play that they use their imaginations in order to comprehend the meaning of what they have seen and heard. One little girl, hospitalized briefly after a car accident, played "hospital" with her friends for months afterwards. It was her way of dealing with and finally putting to rest a frightening event.

Play in the real world is necessary for reading preparation. The more a child experiences the world, the more a book or poem will make sense as it interprets that world. The meaning of a word depends upon previous experience of that word in reality.

The quality of human relationships also depends upon play. Through play, real solutions are found through trial and error or through talking over a problem with other children or an adult. In play with others, conflicts must be resolved. The right words must be called up from one's mind and heart to explain a situation. In the kindergarten, we call it child's play; in our relationships at home or with friends, in business or on the work site, we call it work!

At Home with Your Family

Affirming your child's emerging sense of self-esteem and self-worth is the theme of Lesson 10. The concept that all the wonderful things that I can do are God's gifts to me is developed in Part 2 of the lesson. This is preparation for the child's later understanding that God has made us in his own image and likeness.

Find opportunities to affirm your child's special talents and abilities. Encourage your child to tell you his or her own story from the booklet made in the session. Are there other family members or friends to whom he or she could read the booklet?

Encourage your child to tell you about Alex's favorite things and why they were favorites. Share what your favorite things to taste, see, hear, touch, and smell. Help your child think of and name more of his or her favorite sense experiences.

I Can Do What You Can Do

Have your child enjoy the "I Can Do Game." Have him or her stand facing you. Explain that the purpose of the game is to physically perform a task that you command and to do so as quickly as possible. For example, say, "Jump up and down three times"; "Clap your hands five times"; "Sing a song"; "Take two steps backwards then two steps forward." Congratulate your child on being such a good player.

I Am Special

(*To the tune of "If You're Happy and You Know It"*)

I am special and I know it, clap my hands. (*Clap hands.*)
I am special and I know it, clap my hands. (*Clap hands.*)
I am special and I know it,
And it's oh such fun to show it.
I am special and I know it, clap my hands. (*Clap hands.*)

Second verse:
Let me show you all the things that I can do. (*tap, tap*) . . . .

Learning New Things

See what I have learned.
I can print my first name.

I can count. What number is missing?

  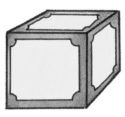

I know the alphabet. What letter is missing?

 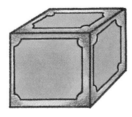 

I can make the sign of the cross.

Use your imagination. Think about one new thing
you will be able to do soon.
Draw what you imagine on another piece of paper.
Tell about your drawing.

I am learning about God.
See what I have learned.

God made __me__ .

God __loves__ me.

God knows my __name__ .

God made our __world__ .

God made __all__ living things.

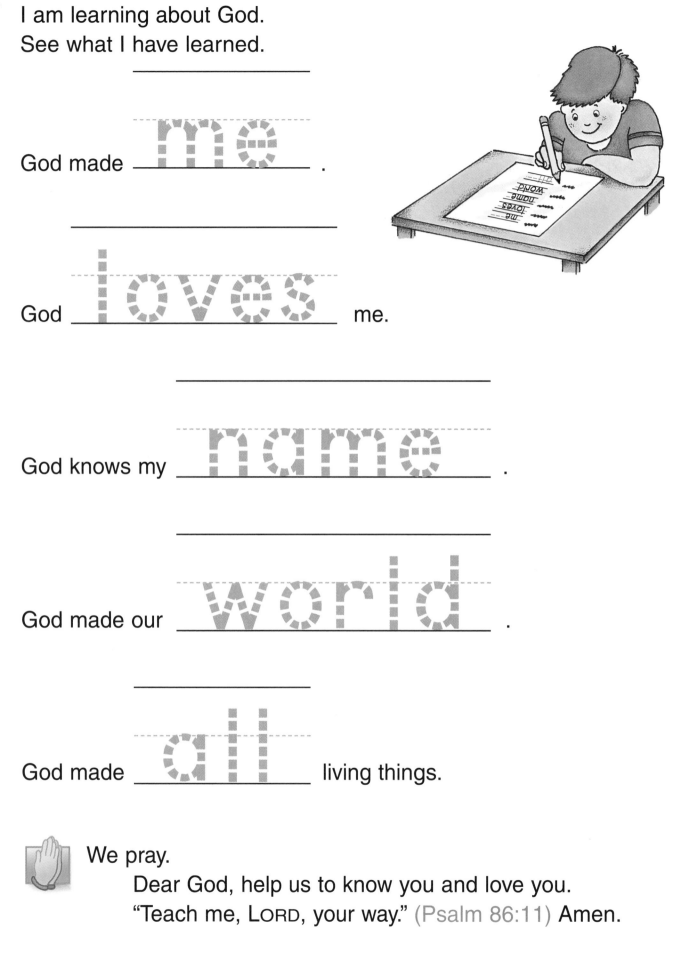

We pray.
Dear God, help us to know you and love you.
"Teach me, LORD, your way." (Psalm 86:11) Amen.

God's Best Gift of All

God loves each one of us more than we can imagine. We belong to God.
God knows each one of us by name.
God gives us many wonderful gifts.

In the Bible we read that God made the world for us.
God made the land and the sea.
God made the animals, plants, and birds for us.
And best of all, God made you and me.

God wants us to know him.
God wants us to love him.
God made us to be happy with him forever.

Then God our Father gave us the best gift of all.
He gave us his own Son, Jesus Christ.
Jesus shows us who God is.
Jesus shows us how to live as God's own children.

Jesus told us to love God with all our hearts.
He also said, "You shall love your neighbor as yourself."

Matthew 22:39

If we live as Jesus shows us, we can be happy with God forever in heaven.
Why did God make us?
How can you show you love God?
How can you show you love your family and friends?

Parenting your 5-Year-Old

Friendship: Gift and Grace

Kindergarten often brings with it a special gift: that of friendship. Friendships made in kindergarten often grow and develop throughout life. Other friendships may last a shorter time but also bring their own gifts of growth.

Through their friendships with other children, fives learn needed skills: acceptance of another way of thinking, the give-and-take of compromise, and the honest realization that sometimes two together can do something that is more fun or more satisfying than just one alone. Independence is good, but interdependence is often better!

> "For he [Christ] is our peace, he who made both one. . . ."
>
> *Ephesians 2:14*

Sometimes these friendships may need adult supervision and mediation, especially if they involve three or more children. The five-year-old can become possessive of "my friend" and may find it difficult to share the friend with someone else or in a group situation.

Five-year-olds are also ready to develop friendships with one or two adults other than the ones with whom they live. Fives enjoy conversations with adults, and may imitate the mannerisms of the cherished grown-up. Whether a neighbor or aunt or uncle, adults who respect the uniqueness of your child should be encouraged to be a part of your child's world.

All our loving relationships are based in God's love for us. With your help, your child will gradually come to understand that each loving relationship in our lives helps us to glimpse God's love and care for us as individuals and in communion with others. The connections we make as friends with one another, brought together by God's loving providence, help us to live as members of the body of Christ. Each friendship is a special grace in our lives that prepares us to respond to God's love more fully and generously. As we learn to give and receive human love, we are at the same time responding to the love that is divine, unconditional, and everlasting.

At Home with Your Family

This lesson continues to deepen the child's sense of self-esteem and self-worth by helping him or her recognize how much has been learned about God. It is important to find the time and opportunity to affirm your child's sense of self-worth. A healthy love of self is foundational to love of neighbor and love of God. As such, it is the key to nurturing and developing a strong, mature life of faith.

You will be delighted as your child shows you how much he or she has learned about God and our world, and imagines what might still be learned.

The *Read to Me* story summarizes the story of creation very simply. The children are introduced to Jesus, the Son of God, who shows us who God is and how God wants us to live. Jesus is the greatest of all the wondrous gifts God has given us.

Share with your child who Jesus is for you. Such modeling and sharing is your gift of faith to your child.

Look at Me Learn

Introduce a few new tasks for your child to try to master.
Folding Clothes: Show your child how to carry a basket of small and/or medium cloth items (such as a handkerchief, hand towel, socks) to a table and fold them, one at a time. Encourage your child to count the folds when working with each individual item.

Watering Plants: Show your child how to care for and water an indoor plant. Point out that certain plants need more watering or sun exposure than others.

I Am Growing
(*To the tune of "Mary Had a Little Lamb"*)

I am growing every day,
Every day,
Every day.
I am growing every day,
And I belong to God.

I am learning how to live,
How to live,
How to live.
I am learning how to live
As a child of God.

Lesson 12
Growing and Changing

In God's world, everything grows and changes.
Tell how plants grow and change.
Put the pictures in the right order.
Mark them 1, 2, 3, or 4.

Act out how animals grow and change.
Act out how birds grow and change.

God has a plan.

In God's plan, plants grow and change.

Animals grow and change.

People grow and change, too.

Put the pictures in the right order.

Mark them 1, 2, 3, or 4.

Cut out these pictures. Make a mobile.

Tell a story about people growing and changing.

 "I shall praise the LORD all my life."

Psalm 146:2

48

God's Plan

"Mom, why doesn't Grandpa come over to play with me like he used to?" asked Ronnie. "I miss him. Doesn't he love me anymore?"

Ronnie's mother hugged him tightly. "Ronnie, your grandfather will always love you but he is very sick. We are all very worried about him."

"Is Grandpa going to die?" Ronnie asked.

Ronnie's mother hugged him even closer. She explained, "We don't know, but we do know that God has a plan for all of us. In God's plan, people are born and they grow up. Someday, everyone has to die. Dying is part of God's plan just like being born. But when we die it is only our bodies that stop living. Usually our bodies are old and tired and sometimes even sick. But the part of us that loves and thinks and feels never dies. Who we really are goes on to live with God forever in heaven."

Ronnie felt better. He thought of all the good times he had with Grandpa—fishing, watching the birds, and listening to all of Grandpa's funny stories. Ronnie knew that, whatever happened, God would take good care of Grandpa always.

Parenting your 5-Year-Old

Celebrating Death and Life

Children will accept death in much the same way as the adults around them accept it. The five-year-old will imitate adults on the occasion of death and will reflect adult attitudes at this difficult time for the family.

Do children belong at wakes and funerals? In discussing this question, it is important for adults to consider what is being said by and to the family at a wake and a funeral. A wake is an opportunity to face the reality of this loved one's death; it is also an opportunity to share memories with friends and relatives. It is an opportunity to share comfort and hope with all of those with whom we and our loved one shared during life. A wake is part of the process of grieving. It is a last chance to show our care for this person whose body we Catholics believe is a temple of the Holy Spirit.

> *"Lord, for your faithful people life is changed, not ended."*
> *Preface of Christian Death I*

A funeral liturgy is a final good-bye, but it is more than that. After all, *good-bye* at its root comes from the English phrase, "God be with you." The entire funeral Mass assures us that God is truly with our loved one, and that, contrary to what we see, "Life is changed, not ended." The funeral liturgy is both an expression of grief and a celebration of life—the earthly life of someone we loved and the eternal life in God's love that we all someday hope to share together.

Five-year-olds do grieve. They are affected by the severe change in relationships that death or other separations bring. They are sensitive to being left out of important family events, and this feeling should be taken into account when deciding whether or not a child could be included at a wake or a funeral. As one little girl said to her family, "I want to say goodbye, too!"

At Home with Your Family

The unit theme of God's plan for us continues to be experienced by your child as he or she discovers the life cycle of plants and animals and then human beings. Encourage your child to tell you the story of the pictures of human growth that he or she has pasted in the correct order. Your child might enjoy looking at some of the clothes outgrown since babyhood. This is a real experience of growth that children truly enjoy.

The *Read to Me* story of Ronnie's very ill grandfather is included here as preparation for understanding God's plan for us. If there has been a death in your child's immediate family, or if he or she has lost a beloved pet, re-reading this story and dialoguing about the concept of being with God forever will be very helpful to your child's growing process. If your child has not yet had such an experience, focus on how much God loves us, that God wants us to be with him forever.

Several excellent books are also available on this topic. Here are a few:

Gellman, Rabbi Marc and Msgr. Thomas Hartman. *Lost & Found: A Kid's Book for Living Through Loss.* New York: Morrow Junior Books, 1999.

Madler, Trudy. *Why Did Grandma Die?* Chatham, NJ: Raintree Steck-Vaughn, 1991.

Shriver, Maria. *What's Heaven?* New York: Golden Books, 1999.

Growing and Changing

Help your child to make a miniature bouquet of flowers to celebrate growing and changing things. You will need several green pipe cleaners for stems, a large spool of colored thread for a vase, and colored kitchen sponges to cut into flowers. Help your child to cut petals into the sponges, making sure the petals remain attached at the center. Push the end of a pipe cleaner through the center of each flower. Bend and place the stems securely into the hole of the spool. Place the bouquet in the center of your table.

God Has a Plan

(*To the tune of "Mary Had a Little Lamb"*)

God has got a plan for me,
Plan for me, plan for me.
God has got a plan for me.
I'm growing every day.

I'm growing in my family,
Family, family.
I'm growing in my family,
And in God's family, too.

To be born, every baby needs a mother and a father.
God gives us life through our mothers and fathers.
Our families love and care for us.
They help us to grow.

Cut out the babies.
Paste them with their mothers and fathers.
Tell how the mothers and fathers
care for their babies.

Families have special stories to tell.

These stories help us know about our families.

Do you have a storyteller in your family? Who is it?

Draw one of your favorite family stories here.

Tell the story of your picture to your family.

Ask someone to tell you another family story.

 We pray.
Dear God, please bless our families.
Help us love one another and be kind
to one another. Amen.

The Holy Family

Jesus had a family, too. Jesus, the Son of God, grew up with his mother, Mary, and Joseph, his foster father. Joseph was a carpenter. He taught Jesus how to use tools to make things out of wood. Jesus liked to do all the same happy things the other children did in the little town where he grew up.

We know that Jesus was a good boy. He always tried to do what Mary and Joseph asked him to do. He loved them very much and helped them in any way he could.

Jesus learned how to love God his Father and how to pray to God with his family. From Mary and Joseph, Jesus learned all the stories of his family. We call Jesus, Mary, and Joseph *the Holy Family.*

We can pray to the Holy Family. We can ask Jesus, Mary, and Joseph to help us love one another.

What things do you learn from your family?

How does your family help you learn about God?

Parenting your 5-Year-Old

Big Brother, Big Sister

The Church teaches that "by transmitting human life to their descendants, man and woman as spouses and parents cooperate in a unique way in the Creator's work" (*Catechism*, 372). This is the privilege and challenge of parenthood—to care for each unique child. For each child has an inner essence, a soul, that will never die; each child has the capacity to love and to be loved; to receive life from others and to nurture life in others; to think, to feel, to make choices.

> "For a child is born to us."
> Isaiah 9:5

Bringing a new baby home is a significant event in the life of the entire family. It may bring up conflicting feelings in your five-year-old: at worst, fear that Mom may not come back from the hospital or perhaps anxiety at her absence; happiness at having a new brother or sister; anger at having to share parents and relatives with a newcomer; pride when the new role of "elder sibling" is recognized and praised.

It is important to reassure big brother or big sister that the new baby will only add to family happiness. The five-year-old's place in the family is secure. Affirm your five's gifts and talents: "You give such great hugs!"

As you welcome your new child, try to spend extra time doing a favorite activity or going on a special outing with your elder child. Sometimes giving the five-year-old his or her own "new baby doll" to care for may help him or her feel closer to Mom, Dad, and the new baby.

Parenthood as cooperation with God does not end with conception and birth. It only begins there. You can rightly tell your elder child that he or she is needed as a sister or brother in the family: "God gave us this baby so that we can help him (her) to grow. Mom helps, and Dad helps, and you can help, too. We can all help each other grow in this family!"

At Home with Your Family

This lesson begins the exploration of the theme of belonging to a family. It is intended to deepen your child's awareness that God's great gifts of life and love come to us through families. The lesson continues to provide a basis for appreciating the Bible as the story of God's family, the Church. The Holy Family is presented so that the children will see within it the model of love, care, and service that is our Christian ideal.

Invite your child to tell you the family story drawn on the *Activity Page*. Tell some of your favorite family stories to one another. Share the story of the Holy Family, allowing quiet time to talk about the questions at the end of the story. Your child might not have thought of the many kindnesses extended to one another in your family as gifts from God, but this would be a good time to point them out.

Here's My Family!

Using paper plates, make a "Family Portrait Gallery" with your child. Collect as many small paper plates as needed to represent a face for each family member. Help your child use marking pens to draw the unique features of each person. Glue yarn or torn pieces of construction paper for hair. Then add bits and pieces of fabric, ribbon, and jewelry for clothing and accessories. Staple a bow above the first plate. Connect the plates with staples and hang as shown in the illustration.

The Holy Family
(*To the tune of "Old MacDonald"*)

Jesus had a family
Just like you and me.
His family loved him oh so much,
Just like mine loves me.

With a clap, clap, here,
And a clap, clap, there,
Here a clap,
There a clap,
Everywhere a clap, clap.
Jesus had a family
Just like you and me.

Lesson 21
Forgiving

Sometimes it is not easy to be kind.
Sometimes we are mean or unkind to
our families or our friends.
Then we need to say, "I am sorry."
People who love us forgive us.
Why do these children need to say, "I am sorry"?

Dear _____,
I am sorry. I love you.

Does someone need to hear you say, "I am sorry"?
Draw how you can show you are sorry.

If we have been unkind or mean
we can show we are sorry.
How are these people showing they are sorry?
Make up a story for each picture card.
Act out ways you can show you are sorry in your family.
Cut out the picture cards and take them home.
Tell someone how you will show you are sorry.

 We pray.
Dear God, help us to say, "I am sorry" and show it
if we have been mean or unkind. Amen.

God Loves Us and Forgives Us

One day Jesus told his friends a wonderful story about being sorry. Here is the story Jesus told.

Once there was a young man who decided to leave his father and run away from home. He went far, far away. At first, he had a lot of fun. He did whatever he felt like doing. But soon, all his money was gone. He was alone and hungry.

One day the young man knew he had done the wrong thing. He was so sorry he had left his father and wasted all his money. He decided to go back home to tell his father how sorry he was.

The father never stopped loving his son. The minute he saw his son coming home, he ran to meet him and hugged him. The son knew he was forgiven. What a wonderful celebration they had!

Jesus wants his friends to know that God is our loving Father. God always loves us and forgives us when we are sorry.

Who always loves you?

Act out how you show, "I am sorry."
Act out how you show, "I forgive you."

Parenting your 5-Year-Old

Forgiveness in Families

It is remarkable that the image of human breath and the work of God in human life are so linked. A powerful image of God's work is given us in the Book of Genesis: God breathes the breath of life into a man of clay "and so man became a living being" (Genesis 2:7). Jesus Christ, the Son of the Father, also brings life in the Spirit through his own living breath, a life and breath he shared first with his disciples and still shares with us.

> Jesus appeared to the disciples, breathed on them, and said, "Receive the holy Spirit."
> John 20:22

Family life is also a sharing of this life-giving breath. This family closeness is life-giving to those who share it on a daily basis.

A sudden shock can "take our breath away" or "knock the wind out of us." On the level of spirit and life, this can happen when one member of the family hurts another in some way. The life-giving breath of the Spirit is suddenly interrupted, even smothered. The simple act of breathing, now gives way to tension, stress, or, in the case of young children, wails and tears.

What restores the breath of life? The giving and receiving of the Holy Spirit through forgiveness.

Forgiveness is not denial that anything ever happened; it is an acknowledgment that something *did* happen that needs attention. Forgiveness is an opportunity for a change of heart in ways large and small. Both the one asking for forgiveness and the one who grants it are faced with human weakness. As Saint Paul wrote, "For I do not do the good I want, but I do the evil I do not want" (Romans 7:19). No one is exempt from this struggle, and only the grace of Jesus Christ can help us through it.

The process of forgiveness allows for a mutual discussion. First, take time to "take a deep breath" and be mindful of the presence of the Holy Spirit. Then the dialogue can begin: "When you did that, I felt hurt." The other may say, "I didn't mean to; I'm sorry."

Children need to hear, overhear, and also participate in this kind of dialogue. True sorrow involves a request and a promise, "Please forgive me. I won't do it again." Finally, there is peace: "Thank you. I do forgive you. Now I can breathe again." "Me, too." (A big hug!)

At Home with Your Family

One of the most difficult skills to be nurtured in children is that of learning to say or show "I am sorry." This lesson helps children become aware of the need to express sorrow for meanness or unkindness. This lesson is also an introduction to the true meaning of forgiveness, a basic understanding at the heart of Christian moral development.

Ask your child to tell you about the card he or she made to be given to someone who needs to hear, "I am sorry." Help your child explore other ways to express sorrow — hugs, notes, kind deeds, and so on.

Remember that the most powerful of all these ideas is learned when you ask your child to forgive you. Do you freely express your regret to your child? Have you ever asked him or her to forgive you?

Has your child seen adults in your family expressing forgiveness? These powerful lessons are best learned young and in the home.

Saying "I Am Sorry"

Make a "Forgive Me Heart" so that your child, along with other members of your family, will have an opportunity to more easily say, "I am sorry." Print the words *I am sorry*, on one side of a heart made from poster board and *Forgive me* on the other side. Glue a magnet strip to one side and stick on the refrigerator door or another metal surface. Encourage your child to use the heart whenever he or she wants to say, "I am sorry."

I Am Sorry
(*To the tune of "London Bridge"*)

I am sorry, yes I am,
Yes I am, yes I am.
I am sorry, yes I am.
Please forgive me.

Didn't mean to hurt you so,
Hurt you so, hurt you so.
Didn't mean to hurt you so.
I do love you.

More About the Bible

We know that God's best gift to us is his Son, Jesus.
In the Bible we read that Jesus said,
"I am the light of the world." (John 8:12)

Color the pictures.
Talk about them with someone you love.

The bright sun reminds
us of Jesus.

The big candle in church
reminds us of Jesus.

We pray.
    Jesus, help us to love God our Father as you did.
    Help us to love one another.
    Amen.

Draw a picture to show what Jesus' message
means to you.

Jesus said, "Love one another
as I love you."
John 15:12

UNIT 4
Growing in the Catholic Church

Parenting your 6-Year-Old

Now We Are Six

The English poet A. A. Milne wrote a book of poetry entitled *Now We Are Six*. The "star" of the book was his own young son, Christopher—the Christopher Robin of the Pooh stories. In this book of poems, Milne captured the world of the six-year-old. Unlike *The House at Pooh Corner* and similar stories, it was no longer a child's imaginary world, revolving around a child. It was an adult world, the real world, seen and participated in from a child's perspective.

> "When I was a child, I used to talk as a child, think as a child, reason as a child; when I became a man, I put aside childish things."
>
> *I Corinthians 13:11*

The six-year-old, while far from being an adult, is beginning "to put aside childish things." The world of the six is no longer confined to the family home, the yard, the park, and the kindergarten. It is or will soon become the elementary school, the other children on the bus, the teacher you may see twice a year, school friends and other parents you may also see infrequently if at all, and even the computer and the Internet.

Your six-year-old is straining forward toward all this and yet reaching back at the same time. Your child is still a child—still talks as a child, thinks as a child, reasons as a child. Yet, because a wider world is calling, your child senses that the scene is shifting. Expectations for the future are in the air.

For the six, the deeper questions are, "Where do I fit in? Will I be okay? Will I do as well as my brothers or sisters or cousins?" These are sometimes unspoken questions and fears, but real.

Spoken or unspoken, these questions and fears demand a parental response of unwavering reassurance. "You'll be fine. We'll always be here for you. We're behind you 100 percent!" No one can predict the future. There may well be challenges ahead. As you prepare your child for the wider world, remember that not all "childish things" can be put away at once, nor should they be. Now that "we are six"—well, six is still *only* six!

Additional Parenting Resources

Hirsch E.D. and John Holdren, editors. *What Your Kindergartner Needs to Know.* New York: Dell Publishing Company Inc., 1997.

Nelson Gertrud Mueller. *To Dance with God: Family Ritual and Community Celebration.* New York/Mahwah: Paulist Press, 1986.

Rosemond, John. *Parent Power: A Common Sense Approach to Parenting in the 90's and Beyond.* Kansas City, MO: Andrews & McMeel, 1991.

At Home with Your Family

The lessons in Unit 4 make more specific the many ways we live in the Church in response to God's love. A lesson on Baptism continues to emphasize one dimension of this first sacrament of initiation as the celebration of belonging to the Church. The beautiful Bible stories of Jesus' great love for us are also continued. A lesson on prayer introduces early learning experiences to encourage your child's emerging relationship with God. Perhaps the most powerful and longlasting lessons about prayer are learned as we pray within our own families. Is prayer becoming a time of closeness and sharing with your child?

Your child's growing awareness of belonging to your parish is further developed in this unit with lessons preparing for participation in the Mass and in the sacraments.

The program concludes with a reflection on the great truth of faith that God's love lasts forever. A final lesson encourages your child to remember God's loving presence during the upcoming summer months. Are there ways you can encourage him or her to respond to God with your family during the summer?

For Storytime During Unit Four

Cronin, Gaynell Bordes and Joan Bellina. *Together at Mass.* Notre Dame, IN: Ave Maria Press, 1987.

Nelson, Gertrud Mueller. *A Walk Through Our Church.* New York/Mahwah: Paulist Press, 1998.

Loving God

I belong to my family.
My family loves me and cares for me.
Because my family loves me so much, they
wanted me to belong to a special family, the Church.
My family brought me to be baptized.
My Baptism was a wonderful celebration.
How happy everyone was!

Write your name on this candle.
It is like the one your family was given
when you were baptized.

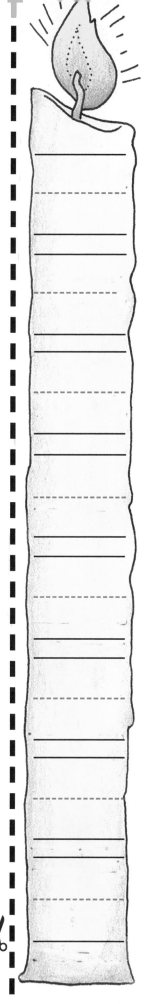

I have been baptized. Baptism made me
a child of God.
I belong to a special family, the Catholic Church.
I am a Catholic.
I have God's own life in me.
Jesus shows me how to live in God's family
and in my family, too.

Decorate and color the candle.
Cut it out to remind you that you are God's child.

Jesus wants us to be his friends.
Jesus said, "Follow me."
John 1:43

A Baptism Celebration

Samantha was so excited! It was her sister Sarah Ann's Baptism day! Samantha could hardly wait to celebrate Sarah Ann's Baptism with their family.

Everyone was up early on Sunday. Sarah Ann's baptismal dress was hanging in the kitchen where Grammy had ironed it the night before. It was so white and lacy. Samantha had worn the very same one when she was baptized. Mom said that this special dress was a sign of God's new and special life.

When Mom came into the kitchen, Samantha asked, "Will our whole family be at the Baptism?"

Her mother answered, "Yes, our whole family will be there, and our parish family, too. Uncle Frank and Aunt Nancy, Sarah Ann's godparents, will be there. Everyone will be happy that Sarah Ann is being baptized and is becoming a child of God."

Then Dad called, "Is everybody ready for Sarah Ann's Baptism? It's time to go!"

The church was full of people. When the time came, the priest baptized Sarah Ann with water, saying, "I baptize you in the name of the Father, and of the Son, and of the Holy Spirit." The priest gave a lighted candle to Sarah Ann's family. This candle was a sign that Sarah Ann was filled with the light of Jesus Christ.

Ask someone to tell you about your Baptism.

Was it a wonderful celebration? Why?

Who are your godparents?

Parenting your 5-Year-Old

Signs of Faith

The human world is a world of communication, of word and symbol. Language alone, rich as it is, cannot convey the fullness of human meaning. For that, we need signs and symbols.

Functional signs are probably the most easily understood in our culture. Traffic signs (orange warning cones, yellow caution signs, red stop signs, green lights) provide an important example. But a sign of faith goes beyond the mere giving of directions. A sign of faith is bigger than we are, and we are invited to enter into its meaning. The Eucharist is such a sign. Every sacrament is such a sign.

The sacrament of Baptism is the first sacrament of initiation. Through Baptism, we become children of God and followers of his Son, Jesus Christ. The words of Baptism coupled with the actual pouring of the water symbolize God's life pouring into his new child, now cleansed and brimming with the new life of the Spirit. The baptismal candle is a symbol of the guiding light of Christ shining in this new life.

> "At present I know partially; then I shall know fully, as I am fully known."
>
> *I Corinthians 13:12*

Catholics use *sacramentals* to remind us of our life in God and to prepare us for the graces of the sacraments. Sacramentals are holy objects such as crucifixes, rosaries, holy water, blessed candles, and statues. Sacramentals can also be actions, such as the sign of the cross, the laying on of hands, the sprinkling of blessed water, and the act of blessing. Unlike the sacraments, these sacramentals do not bring about what they signify, but are important reminders to us of the life we have in Christ.

When you introduce your child to these sacramentals, perhaps the simplest explanation is the best. These are signs of God's love for us. When we use them, we are praying to God and thanking God for all he has given us. You may want to introduce the custom of blessing your child each morning or evening. With your right thumb, trace the sign of the cross on your child's forehead and say an appropriate blessing, such as: "May God bless you and give you joy and peace!"

At Home with Your Family

This lesson was planned to help your child discover that at Baptism each of us is welcomed into a special family, the Church. The joy of your family and the parish family is highlighted so that your child can experience the unique importance of Baptism in our journey of faith.

The candle is introduced in this lesson. Can you find a prominent place in your home to display the candle your child made? Did you save his or her baptismal candle?

Invite your child to retell the story of the Baptism of Samantha's new sister from the illustrations on the *Read to Me* page. Do you have any pictures, mementos, or stories of your child's Baptism that you could share? Sharing such stories and treasures is a valuable element in your child's growing awareness of belonging to the Catholic Church.

Baptism "Show and Tell"

Celebrate your child's Baptism by having a "Show and Tell Game." You will need a box with a removable lid topped with a bow. Each family member should place in the box something that has special significance in the life of your child: for example, your child's baptismal certificate, baby pictures, and so on. Each family member then takes out an object and tells your child about its significance.

My Baptism
(*To the tune of "Mary Had A Little Lamb"*)

I became a child of God,
Child of God, child of God.
I became a child of God
On my Baptism day.

Jesus said, "Come, follow me,
Follow me, follow me."
Jesus said, "Come, follow me"
On my Baptism day.

Lesson 27
Talking to God

Tell what is happening in these pictures.
Who is talking? Who is listening?

Who talks to you? Who listens to you?
Draw who talks and listens to you on another paper.
Tell about your drawing.

We like to talk to and listen to people we love.
God loves us. We can talk to and listen to God.
We can pray to God in our own words.
Here are some things we can say
to God when we pray.

Finish the prayers. Decorate them.
Cut them out.
Use them to help you pray to God each day.

✂

Dear God,
please help me
to live as
your child. Amen.

Thank you,
God, for all
your gifts. Amen.

I am sorry,
God, if I have
been mean. Amen.

Dear God,
how wonderful
you are.
I love you. Amen.

We Pray to God

"Thank you, thank you, thank you, God,"
We say in prayer each day.
Thank you for the gifts you give.
Thank you, God, we pray.

"Help us, help us, help us, God,"
We say in prayer each day.
Help us live the way you say.
Help us, God, we pray.

"We're sorry, sorry, sorry, God,"
We say in prayer each day.
We're sorry when we have done wrong.
We're sorry, God, we pray.

"We love you, love you, love you, God,"
We say in prayer each day.
How wonderful you are, dear God.
We love you more each day.

Make up a prayer to God.
What will you say?
Pray your prayer with someone
in your family.

Parenting your 5-Year-Old

Talking and Listening

If prayer is defined as "talking to and listening to God," then it really does not seem that difficult. After all, we talk to and listen to people all the time, and how hard is that?

Truthfully, it is very hard. Caring about others involves "walking a mile in their moccasins" (as a Native American saying has it) and sometimes we find that the shoe is not an easy fit. Speaking and listening with clarity and attention is not all that common, with people or with God.

> "With all prayer and supplication, pray at every opportunity in the Spirit."
>
> Ephesians 6:18

However, it is in speaking and in listening that your child learns to pray. The words of both informal and formal prayers are first heard, then repeated, then "learned by heart," and then finally spoken to God in sincerity and truth.

Underneath the talking and listening of family prayer is something very important: an attitude of prayer. This attitude is a reality of faith. It reflects the reality of God in family life: that God is truly with us. One wise woman used to remark, when a friend brought a problem to her: "Hmm. Sounds like something to talk over with God." Sometimes the presence of God is most aptly reflected in silence. We often think of silence as a break in communication, but sometimes, among people and with God, it can be a means of communication.

If a family has made room occasionally for companionable times of reading together, or walking in a park, or listening to the birds, or watching a sunset, then that family is teaching the communicative silence that opens to prayer. Just doing chores together without feeling the need to make conversation can be an experience of prayer.

It is within this context of silent listening that our words will truly mean something. In this American culture, in which children are in danger of becoming constantly overstimulated and yet isolated in front of TV and computers, a little quiet family time may need to be part of an overall plan. One mother, in observing a school-sponsored "No TV Week," responded positively to it: "We rediscovered books. We got out board games. We had time to find out what the others were thinking." Hmm. Sounds like something to talk over with God!

At Home with Your Family

Throughout this program your child has been offered many varied experiences of prayer. The children were taught that prayer is talking to and listening to a loving God and saying what is in their hearts.

The prayer cards your child made and the poem on the *Read to Me* page provide learning experiences for helping him or her appreciate the different kinds of prayer. You might want to invite your child to tell you the story of the different things we can say to God when we pray. Perhaps at bedtime this week you may want to encourage your child to choose one of the prayer cards and pray this kind of prayer as a bedtime prayer. Encouragement from a prayerful parent is the strongest lesson about praying your child can learn.

Learning a Special Prayer

Introduce your child to litanies as a form of prayer. For example:

Leader: I love bright red apples and sunny oranges.

Response: Thank you, God, for your many gifts.

Leader: It's fun playing ball with my friends.

Response: Thank you, God, for your many gifts.

Once your child has mastered the idea, plan to have a litany at bedtime or before mealtime so that all family members can participate.

We Pray to God

(*To the tune of "Mary Had a Little Lamb"*)

Thank you, thank you, thank you, God;
Thank you, God; thank you, God.
Thank you, God, we pray each day.
Thank you, God, we pray.

We love you, love you, love you, God;
Love you, God; love you, God.
How wonderful you are, dear God.
We love you more each day.

Lesson 28
Celebrating in Our Parish Family

Our parish family comes together
for wonderful celebrations.
We meet with other Catholic families who
belong to our parish.
Here are some things we see
in our parish church.
Cut them out. Paste them
in the right places.

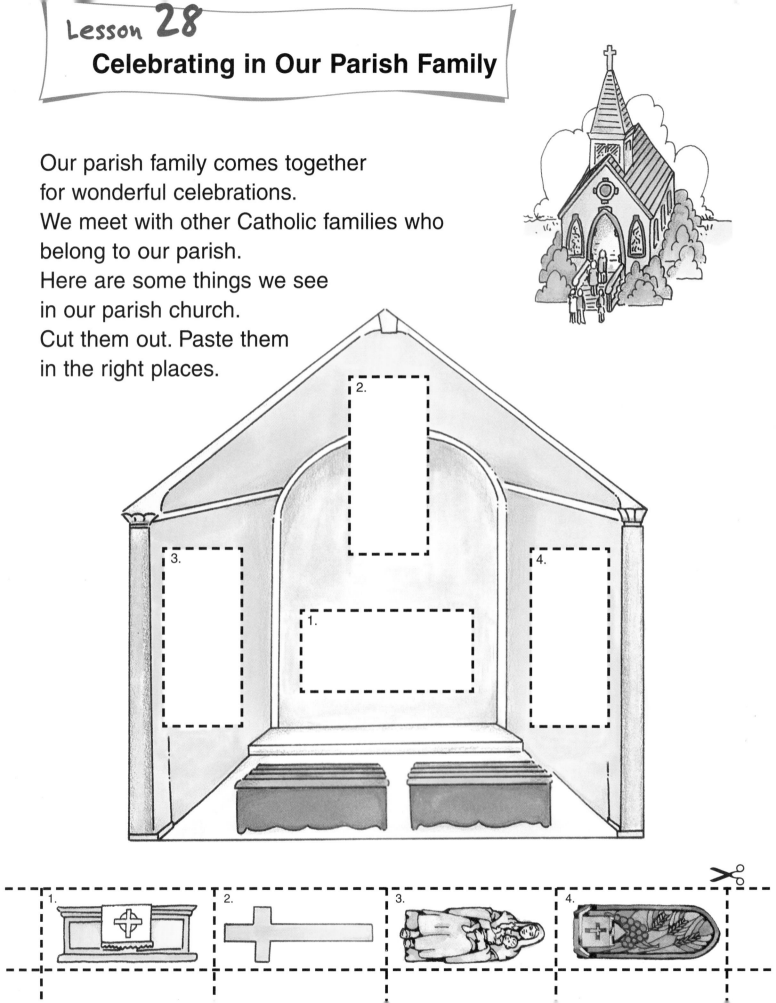

In the Catholic Church, we celebrate
together at Mass.
At Mass we praise God. We thank God.
We celebrate Jesus and the new life
he gives us.

At Mass, the priest is the leader of
our celebration.
We all have a part in the Mass.
Cut out some of the things we do at Mass.
Paste them in the right places.

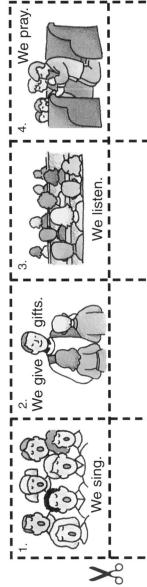

4. We pray.

3. We listen.

2. We give gifts.

1. We sing.

We Celebrate the Mass

Here is how Catholics take part in the Mass.

We pray to God together.

God speaks to us.

We receive Jesus in Holy Communion.

We give gifts to God.

What do you do at Mass?
Can you join in the singing?
Can you join in the prayers?

113

Parenting your 5-Year-Old

Celebrating Sunday

Whether celebrated on Saturday night or on Sunday, the weekly Eucharist structures the weekend. Family activities revolve around this gathering in which we listen to the word of God and share the Bread of life. It is small wonder that your five-year-old is curious about this weekly event that is so important to everyone.

We bring all of ourselves, all of our lives, all of our joys and sorrows to this gathering, where they are caught up into the life of the community and, indeed, the life of Christ. If we realize that we are in relationship with God all the time, not just on Sunday, we are more ready to bring our whole lives with us when we join as a community to express that relationship.

Each Mass is a great event that must be given some thought and preparation ahead of time. For example, your child should be familiar with the parish church. If not, take time to give a little "tour" on a Saturday or another time when the church is open. Your child will imitate your reverence for the church itself and for the Blessed Sacrament. This is an opportunity to explain what all the various symbols and furnishings mean. Perhaps a meeting

> "LORD, I love the house where you dwell, the tenting-place of your glory."
> *Psalm 26:8*

with the parish priest or other ministers could be arranged.

Religious books, including a few books about the Mass, can easily be made part of your child's collection. Perhaps one or two special ones can be saved for the Mass itself. Challenge your child to match the pictures in the book with the actual parts of the Mass. Occasionally whisper a reminder or explanation of what is happening: "See? The priest is offering our gifts of bread and wine to God." Choose a place near the altar if possible, as the back of the church is very unengaging for a child.

Above all, explain to your child that we go to church to give praise and thanks to God, all together, because we are his people. We can pray by our words (in prayer and song) and our actions (standing, kneeling, sitting and listening). We can also pray quietly in our hearts. The weekly Eucharist should not become an endurance test for a child. If your child needs a break for awhile, try not to treat it as a punishment but just as something needed for now.

At Home with Your Family

Throughout this program, experiences have been provided to help your child prepare to participate in the Mass. This lesson summarizes many of these experiences and provides a gentle framework for attitudes and understanding that will later develop.

To make the experience concrete and more meaningful, take the *Activity Page* for this lesson with you when you visit the church with your child. Point out the features of the interior of the church that your child has learned about with the group.

We Are the Church

Help your child to find and cut out pictures of people representing our universal, worldwide family of God. Cut the top portion of a large rectangle of construction paper in the shape of a triangle. This will represent the steeple of a church building. With a crayon, have your

child draw in the doors, windows, and the cross on the top. Paste the pictures of all God's people on the other side of your parish "church."

We Celebrate the Mass
(*To the tune of "Three Blind Mice"*)

Celebrate! Celebrate!
Come to the Mass!
Come to the Mass!
We pray, we listen, give thanks to God
For all of the gifts he has given to us,
Especially Jesus, the Son of God.
Come celebrate! Celebrate!

Summer is almost here.
Find all the things you can do in the summer.
Color them. Tell about them.

God our Father is always with us.
God is with us wherever we go.

115

God loves us always.
God's love will last forever.
We can be with God forever in heaven.

We will always remember
how much God loves us.
Here are some things you know about God.

Use them to help you remember to show
you love God during the summer.

God loves us.

God made the world for us.

God made us to be like him.

God gives us Jesus.

I am God's child.

We Show We Love God

The Barry family is taking a trip during their summer vacation. Imagine you are going with them.

How can they show they love God while they are on their vacation?

Tell how you can show you love God during the summer.

What will you do?

FAMILY CAMPGROUNDS WELCOME

Parenting your 5-Year-Old

On the Road to....

Some adults have fond memories of the mellow days of summer—long days of going barefoot in sprinklers, finding shells in the sand, or making crafts under the trees of a neighborhood park.

Parents today find that summer is more complicated than that. While their children may be on vacation, parents are not! Changes in child care, with new schedules, new play groups, and new day camp arrangements are now a significant part of "summer vacation." Try to prepare your child for these changes ahead of time. With your child, pay a visit to the new group or new babysitter before your child actually starts a new schedule.

> "I will cut a road through all my mountains, and make my highways level."
>
> *Isaiah 49:11*

If you are planning a long vacation trip, especially in the confinement of a car, remember that, for a five-year-old, the journey is just as important as the arrival. Your child should have a small bag of favorite toys and activities to take along: books, paper, crayons, magnet boards, and even simple hand-craft projects. You may want to begin the tradition of having a "bag of tricks" ready for long car trips and visits. In this bag would go surprises to bring out when the familiar toys no longer appeal. Surprises might include juice boxes and snacks, drawing paper with markers, a cassette player with story tapes, or wooden puzzles in frames. This bag can be added to along the way as needed. And don't forget your child's favorite stuffed animal or sleeping pillow!

These smaller journeys, with all their practical details, remind us that, for Christians, life itself is a journey, a journey with God. We Christians are a people moving forward. Like the disciples of Emmaus, we meet Jesus on the road. Whether it be on the road across country or on the road to the grocery store, we share the encouragement of our faith and the companionship of others along the way. May the end of this kindergarten journey be only the beginning of a new journey in growth and love for you and your child!

At Home with Your Family

As your family anticipates the summer season and as this program draws to a close, your child's natural delight in the pleasures of summer was highlighted. The activities for this lesson were planned as a review of the great truths of our faith that the children were helped to experience in the program. Can you find a prominent place to display your child's *Activity Page*? Invite him or her to tell you the story of how much God loves each one of us that is told in the vignettes.

Remembering God's love and responding to God's love during the summer months was the theme of the maze activity. Are you planning a vacation this summer that you can discuss with your child? How do you anticipate remembering God's love for you and your family on that trip and throughout the summer months?

God Is Always With Us

Because summer is a perfect time for planting and watching things grow, help your child make several simple indoor gardens to nurture and observe. For example: Grow a potato plant. Stick four toothpicks around the biggest end of the potato and place it partially in a jar of water. The potato will soon be a trailing potato vine.

Watch beans grow. Place a damp piece of cloth over the top of a jar or glass. Keep the cloth moist. Lay a few large dry beans on top. The beans will soon grow sprouts.

Goodbye and Hello
(*To the tune of "Goodnight Ladies"*)

Goodbye, Kindergarten. Goodbye, Kindergarten.
Goodbye, Kindergarten, for summertime is here!

Hello, Summer! Hello, Summer!
Hello, Summer! It's good to see you here.

(*To the tune of "Merrily We Roll Along"*)

We will play out in the sun,
In the sun, in the sun.
We will play out in the sun,
For summertime is here!

God is with us every day,
Every day, every day.
God is with us every day
And in the nighttime, too.
(*Repeat verses 1 and 2.*)

Mother's Day

Our mothers give us a wonderful gift.
Mothers bring us into life.
Mothers love and care for us.
Other people love us and care for us, too.
We say thank you on Mother's Day.
What gift would you like to give
on Mother's Day?
Draw it on this card.
What can you paste on your card to
make it beautiful?

My gift to you.

Happy Mother's Day

(fold)

God gives us life through our families.
God loves and cares for us
through our families.
Who loves and cares for you?
Draw that person or persons here.
Cut out your card. Give it with
a kiss on Mother's Day.

 We pray.
Thank you, God, for mothers.
Thank you for people who love and care for us.
Amen.

I love you,

(fold)

(your name)

Father's Day

Fathers and mothers give us the gift of life.
Fathers love us and help care for us.
Other people love us and care for us, too.
They show us how to do things.
They help us grow up in our families.
What gift would you like to give on Father's Day?

Draw it on this card. What can you paste on
your card to make it a beautiful gift?

My gift to you

Happy
Father's
Day

(fold)

God's love comes to us through our families.
Who brings you God's love? Draw that person here.
Cut out your card. Give it and say
"thank you" on Father's Day.

 We pray.
Thank you, God, for fathers.
Thank you for those who help us to love you. Amen.

✂ -

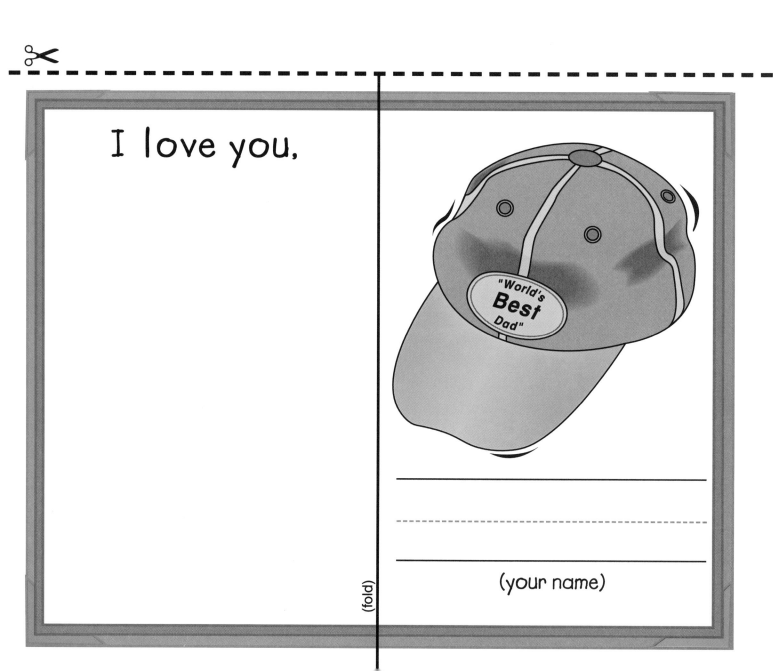

I love you,

(fold)

"World's Best Dad"

(your name)

Mary Is Our Mother

God asked Mary to be the mother
of Jesus. Mary trusted God.
She always lived as a child of God.
Mary said yes to God.
Jesus was born on Christmas Day.
Here is a picture of Mary for you to keep.
What will you say to Mary?

(fold)

Mary, the mother of Jesus, is our mother, too.
Mary knows and loves each one of us.
We can ask Mary to help us and care for us.

When can you pray to Mary?
Cut out your picture of Mary. It can
help you remember to pray to her.

Hail Mary

Hail Mary, full of grace,
the Lord is with you!
Blessed are you among women,
and blessed is the fruit
of your womb, Jesus.
Holy Mary, Mother of God,
pray for us sinners,
now and at the hour of our death.
Amen.

(fold)

Happy Birthday!
This is your special day!

Decorate your birthday cake.
Cut out the candles.
Put as many as you need on your cake.

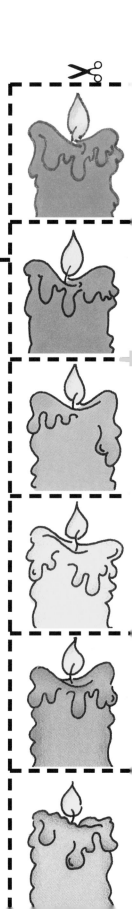

125

The gift of life comes from God.
We celebrate God's gift of life
on our birthdays.

Draw what special things you
will do on your birthday.
Cut out your birthday cake. Take it
home to help celebrate your special day.

 We pray.
Thank you, God, for your gift of life.
Amen.